M000019664

For
Saundra
with a loving
heart.

For Annie

Introduction

Most of us are can-do people. We know what we can do to live more balanced and satisfying lives.

Too few of us are will-do people, people who will do what it takes to realize our dreams, form deep, meaningful connections with others, and embrace the beauty of the world around us.

Highly effective women are will-do women, and we see them every day—at work, in the supermarket, on TV, down the block. They are the women who walk with a confident gait and a

winning smile. Life, they know, is not a dress rehearsal but a grand adventure, a story that unfolds with each sunrise, a story that they themselves write.

You, too, can become a highly effective woman; you, too, can become the author of your life. There's no secret to it. No special genes are required at birth. As this book reveals, all you need is a willingness to listen to your inner compass—your heart of hearts—to truly understand who you are and who you have yet to be. True effectiveness, you'll learn, is essentially a matter of alignment, a wedding of your values and dreams to your actions.

Consider this book, then, a wedding ceremony of sorts. Let its reflections create a union between your goals and reality. Absorb its wisdom and you'll become like the highly effective women you see around you—a will-do woman you truly admire.

◆ B. M. C.

I have an everyday religion
that works for me: Love
yourself first and everything
else falls into line.

❀ Lucille Ball

Highly effective women know that they're not perfect—what work in progress is? Still, they accept themselves, blemishes and all. They know that you can't love life if you don't love yourself first.

You are your dearest and oldest friend, the only being who has been with you each and every moment from the very beginning of your life. You alone know the depths of your heart, the dreams you hold sacred, and all that you can be.

Starting today, strive to be an even better friend to yourself. Treat yourself

with the respect, kindness, and support you deserve. Celebrate your
uniqueness, embrace your faults. Set
an example for how you want others
to treat you.

Do these things and the journey
that is life becomes more interesting
and joyful. Best of all, no matter
where you go, you'll never be alone.
Your loving friend will always be at
your side, cheering you on each step
of the way.

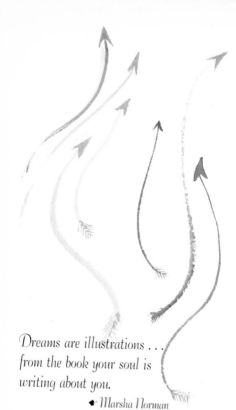

Dreams are illustrations . . .
from the book your soul is
writing about you.

◆ Marsha Norman

Dreams swirl around us like the wind, difficult to grasp and make our own. Still, they awaken something deep within us. They remind us that we can and must do more.

Highly effective women know that dreams are guides that lead to the authentic self. That's why they listen to the whispers of their souls. Dreams, they've learned, are the basis for meaningful action. Dreams infuse life with purpose and propel us forward. They are not to be dismissed or relegated to some remote corner of our minds.

You can be a dreamer. Begin by

drawing your longings closer to your heart. Try to put into words what you want and why. Don't worry about the how; it will come later.

Should words escape you, simply note your feelings. Often we know what we want before we can speak of it. We are filled with a sudden longing to study a new language or grow roses. We feel a hunger for new relationships or a determination to return to school. These out-of-the-blue urges may make no sense, yet they feel right, and it is this "rightness" that lets us know we have hit a bull's-eye.

Today, now, if only for a moment, draw back your bow and let your arrow fly. Let yourself dream and find your target.

No self-respecting, swashbuckling buccaneer would set out in search of buried treasure without a map. Why should you?

★ Sarah Ban Breathnach

Maps serve a variety of purposes. They help us determine direction and distance, guide us through unfamiliar territory, and keep us from getting lost.

But maps are useful only if they take us where we want to go. Follow a map that others have laid out for you or one which distances you from your dreams, and you'll quickly lose interest and perhaps your self-respect.

Highly effective women know that the best maps are those sketched by hand and heart. Such maps help them find true north, measure how far they've journeyed, and how much further they've yet to go. They know that no map can mark every vista and detour, every twist and turn in the road. Still, they use their maps to move forward, pausing when necessary to replenish, re-evaluate, and rejoice.

What is your ultimate destination? What treasures do you envision will await you when you arrive, and which can you enjoy along the way? How do you want to travel, and with whom? What strengths can you draw on to shelter you from occasional but in-evitable storms?

Now that you know more of your innermost dreams, it is time to create your map. Note the direction you want your life to take; sketch out the various routes you can take to reach your goal. Remember: all journeys begin with that first, definitive step. Now is the time to take it and to let your magical journey begin.

I have learned, as a rule of thumb,
never to ask whether you can do
something. Say, instead, that you are
doing it. Then fasten your seat belt.
The most remarkable things follow.

◆ Julia Cameron

We may be students of life, but we're not necessarily in a formal school. We don't have to raise our hands for permission to speak or leave the room. We can—indeed must—act on our own accord.

Highly effective women know that they can't always wait for permission to move forward, nor can they expect the blessings of others, even those they love. They are willing to proceed toward their authentic selves.

Visualize the changes you'd like to make in your life. What stops you from taking action? Are you raising your hand, seeking permission, waiting for others to accept your needs, even though they may prefer the status quo? Are you stuck in place because you keep asking yourself if you're capable of undertaking a new venture, learning a new skill, opening your heart to a special someone? If so, know that such questions are akin to asking permission and that in doing so you give up the power to determine your future.

Empower yourself by making your future your present. Imagine that you are already doing what you long to do. Breathe it, smell it, touch it. Know that it can and will be yours when you give yourself permission to accept it. Then open your arms in welcome. Wonderful changes are coming your way.

Allow things to be meaningful and they become meaningful.

◆ *Laura Day*

In life, there are no right or wrong answers; there are only our interpretations of what we see, experience, believe.

Highly effective women know that to a great extent they frame their own realities. They know that their interpretations are the filters through which they view the world.

See yourself as courageous, loving, and free-spirited. See the world as grand, beautiful, supportive, and magical—and it becomes so.

Seeing things in this way doesn't make you immune to life's disappointments or to the sting of another's sharp words. Nor does it mean that you'll be able to banish all doubts and fears from your mind. It does mean that you will have the final say, the last word in your conversations with yourself. You will have the power to change your world, to turn negative thoughts and experiences into golden learning opportunities.

Developing this power takes practice and conscious effort. You must train yourself to see the glass as half full, remind yourself to carry around your rose-colored glasses. That's why you must get in the habit of discovering life's daily treasures. Put a new spin on

old ways of thinking. Turn disempow-
ering thoughts into empowering ones.
Most importantly, accept the role you
play in creating your reality by making
your life meaningful on your own,
positive terms.

BLADES OF GRASS

To me, working is a form of suste-
nance, like food or water, and
nearly as essential.

◆ Katharine Graham

*H*ighly effective women know that work doesn't have to be, well, such hard work. It also should be fun.

Fun, for them, takes many forms. It's learning a new skill or knowledge area. It's interacting with others to achieve a shared goal. It's making a valuable and lasting contribution in the workplace.

Highly effective women know that their professional and personal lives are expressions of the same being, a being who wants to live her life to the fullest.

There's no need to put your special

talents and strengths on hold from 9 to 5, or to work a dead-end job that leaves you feeling dead at the end of the day. Work is play in the game of life. It is as important as the air you breathe, sustaining your spirit and making possible other adventures.

How you make a living says much about the life you are living. That's why it's essential that you find work that engages your thoughts, captures your heart, and inspires you to do what only you can do.

To find meaningful work, you must first determine what is meaningful to you. What would your ideal job be like? What hours would you prefer to work and with whom? What types of projects or products most appeal to you? In what arena or setting would you blossom most fully?

These questions may not be easy to answer, but they will help you answer the most important question of all: what do you want your work life to say about you?

*Flops are a part of
life's menu and I've
never been a girl to
miss out on any of
the courses.*

◆ Rosalind Russell

*H*ighly effective women have a hearty appetite for life. They fill their plates with rich experiences and inspirational dreams. They, like us, want it all—happiness, success, security, and inner peace. But they also understand that life is a package deal. It has its ups and downs, not to mention in-betweens.

Failures, like successes, are also part of life. Failures may not be fun, but they do serve a purpose. Sometimes they indicate that the direction we're taking is leading us away from our authentic selves. Other times they indicate that we are trying to do too much, too soon, or that we first need additional knowledge or skills.

What failures *do not* indicate is that we, ourselves, are failures, or that our efforts are futile. In fact, the only way to ensure that we fail is to never try to succeed: We lose each and every time by default.

Think of so-called failures in your life. What gifts did each present in terms of lessons learned or experiences earned? How did they help you evolve into the being you are today? In what positive ways are they helping you redefine your goals and the means for accomplishing them? How can you

use them to more fully enjoy the ban-
quet that is life with its many and
varied courses? Count every lesson
that you learn as a success.

Just as physical pain
tells us to take our
hand off the hot
stove, the pain of
our anger preserves
the very integrity of
our self.

◆ Harriet Goldhor
Lerner

Anger may be among the least popular of emotions, but its presence in our lives is inevitable—and necessary.

As highly effective women know, anger serves many functions. It signals when we feel hurt or taken advantage of, or when certain behaviors (be they in ourselves or others) become intolerable. Anger forces us out of our complacency, propelling us to effect long-overdue changes, and gives us the energy we need to take on new challenges. Ultimately, it is a window through which we can see our authentic selves.

Too often, we bury our anger in denial and guilt. We buy into the notion that we should remain cool, calm, collected—and nice. Well, nice girls may not get angry, but highly effective women do. They accept the legitimacy of their emotions and their right to express them. And they do so in constructive ways. Anger, they've learned, is not a weapon, but a tool with which to build a life of integrity.

How can you use anger to your advantage? You begin by acknowledging its presence in your life. Where, when, and how often does it crop up? Next, consider the message your anger is trying to deliver. Is your authentic self telling you to change your circumstances, circle of friends, or approach? Or is it merely asking that you re-evaluate your expectations or assert your needs?

Finally, weigh your possible courses of action. How, for example, can you turn a seemingly unlivable situation into a livable one? What is the best way to get what you want without denying the wants of others? How might a shift in your attitude or perspective help dissipate negative feelings? In what ways can you use your anger to support your growth and make your world a better place?

Finding blame does not find solutions.

● *Laura Schlessinger*

*H*ighly effective women know how to resist temptation—and one of life's greatest temptations is to place blame.

Placing blame is an easy way out. It's a way to wrap hurt, anger, and disappointment into neat little packages and lay them at someone else's feet.

But laying blame, though convenient, doesn't make life easier. To blame is to shun responsibility, to refuse to accept the consequences of our actions or inactions, be they intentional or not. Worse, blame freezes us in space and time. It is a reaction that focuses on the who and what rather than on the why or how. We are so busy passing the buck that we fail to consider ways to prevent similar situations or interactions from occurring in the future. More sadly, we fail to heal our wounds and our relationships with others.

Highly effective women seek solutions, not blame. Rather than pointing a finger of blame, they extend a hand in peace, friendship, and respect. They accept their role in a situation and strive to move on and beyond negative emotions.

Whenever you feel the urge to blame someone or something for your predicament, take a deep breath and visualize at least one thing that you, and you alone, could do to alter the outcome. Perhaps it's a matter of changing your expectations or the tone of your voice, becoming a better listener, or completing a long-overdue task, however unpleasant. Seize the opportunity.

Don't worry about saving face or having another meet you halfway. Rather, focus your energies on moving on and beyond to higher ground.

The body is a sacred garment. . . .
it should be treated with honor.
◆ *Martha Graham*

The sweet chatter of birds greeting the day . . . the awesome beauty of a fiery sunset . . . the wondrous smell of cookies in the oven . . . the profound softness of a loved one's embrace. These are but some of the many joys we experience, all of which are made possible by our bodies.

Highly effective women know that our bodies are sacred garments that must be worn with pride. They don't waste their time moaning and groaning about imperfect features; that would be an act of disrespect. The body, after all, is a gift, given to each of us at birth. Without it, we could not move through time and space. We could not know the world or ourselves.

Like any sacred object, the body must be treated with care. It requires adequate rest, exercise, and a healthful diet to give it the ability to handle the stresses and activities of everyday life.

Just as importantly, it needs our friendship. It needs to be greeted in the mirror with a smile, not a frown; to be accepted on its own terms, rather than held to a questionable ideal. It wants, as we all do, to be loved.

Think of the many loving ways you can show your body your appreciation.

Go for an invigorating walk before work. Reach for a nourishing fruit instead of a candy bar when the afternoon doldrums hit. Play dress-up, using bright colors and festive prints to draw attention to the beauty of your body. Look in the mirror and say "thanks." Better yet, give yourself a heartfelt hug.

There are some things you learn best in
calm, and some in storm.

◆ Willa Cather

Change can be like a storm—unsettling, forceful, seemingly beyond our control. No wonder we often run from it, seeking shelter in the familiar. Change, however, is one of life's constants. Natural and necessary, it leads us to a greater understanding of ourselves.

Wouldn't it be nice if change came at our beck and call, whenever we felt ready, willing, and able to welcome it? Wouldn't it also be nice to have it move at the pace with which we felt most comfortable?

Change, of course, has a mind of

her own. She's a teacher who designs her own lesson plans, and whether we are willing or not, we have no choice but to learn from her. And to grow.

Highly effective women are committed to embracing life's lessons. They know that some lessons are learned in calm, others in storm, but that all present unique opportunities for growth.

What opportunities await you today? What changes deserve your embrace rather than your resistance? What can you do to become a better student, to master the lessons life has so graciously set before you?

We usually live in the realm of second
or third thoughts, thoughts on
thoughts, rather than in the realm of
first thoughts, the real way we flash
on something.

◆ Natalie Goldberg

Highly effective women are jugglers extraordinaire. They juggle the many roles they play yet still seem to maintain their sense of balance. But how?

By taking the time to center themselves. They know that to live a full, active life, they must have solitary, quiet moments. They must go within to gain strength, momentum, perspective.

We, too, need down time to pick ourselves up. We need an opportunity to hear ourselves think and feel.

Too often, however, our authentic selves get lost in the shuffle of

everyday life. We are barraged by inter-
ruptions, to-do lists, deadlines, and
the demands of others. As a result, we
become distant from our "first
thoughts," those wondrous flashes of
insight and inspiration that illuminate
our souls.

You need not run off to a secluded
cabin to commune with yourself (nice
as that would be!) or to meditate for
hours on end. All you need is a few
moments each day to write in a jour-
nal, take a leisurely walk, or relax in a
comfortable chair. The key is to create
a sacred time during which you let
your mind wander wherever it chooses
to go. Give it the opportunity, and it

will make a beeline for first thoughts.

Hold these first thoughts near and dear. Use them as a reminder of what is truly important in life. Over time, you will find it easier to align your actions and values, and to return, at last, to your authentic self.

The great thing about getting
older is that you don't lose all the
other ages you've been.

◆ Madeleine L'Engle

*H*ighly effective women do not worry about the passage of time or opportunities lost. They live in the present, where life, like a ripe fruit, is at its sweetest. And most real.

We, too, must embrace the present. Here, now, with each passing moment, we can add to the treasure chest that is our lives.

Through the years we've accumulated so many valuables—loving friends, favorite belongings, poignant experiences, important insights. They are ours forever and always, close as our hearts and minds. These riches have made us who we are, and as we continue to evolve, we will add even more of them to our treasure chest.

Take a moment to think of the treasures that are in your life. Consider, for example, a once-dear friend and the closeness you shared when you were younger. Remember the heart-felt talks, the laughter, the tears. Think of the many gifts that that friendship offered and how each, in turn, helped you become in small or large part the person you are today.

In much the same way, ponder the highs and lows of your past . . . old loves and hates . . . previous jobs and places you have lived. Note how each has shaped you, made you stronger, deeper, wiser. Where would you be—indeed who would you be—without these treasures?

We need love in order to live
happily, as much as we need
oxygen in order to live at all.
◆ *Marianne Williamson*

To live, we must fill our lungs with oxygen—and our hearts with love.

Love gives life meaning, dimension, a special glow. It transforms the ordinary into the extraordinary, and brightens our darkest days and thoughts. Without love, we are incomplete, unable to embrace life's gifts or to give of ourselves.

Highly effective women know that love comes in all shapes, sizes, and intensities, and that all are important to our well-being. There is the love of significant relationships, which provide great comfort and opportunities for growth. There is the love of challenging works, which enable us to contribute to the world. There is the love of favorite pursuits—curling up with a book, taking a luxurious bath, sharing a laugh with a friend—that make life so rich and fun.

Highly effective women expect—indeed demand—that love permeate their lives. And so should we. Life is too short not to be lived deeply, passionately. Love should be part of our everyday and every-moment lives.

What do you love in life? What makes your heart sing? Fresh-cut flowers? Intimate candlelit dinners? Anything and everything pink? Draw those things to you. Drop by the florist on your way home from work. Set a date for your next culinary rendezvous. Wrap a hot pink scarf around your waist when you run errands.

Think, too, of the special people you love having in your life: the soulmate who always knows when you need a hug, the special friend who makes each get-together a hilarious adventure, the mentor who inspires you by example. Express your thankfulness for their love. Present them with a small but special gift—a handmade card, a heart-felt poem, a bear hug. Celebrate their presence in your life by making your life a celebration of love. ❦